THE ESCORIAL

THE ROYAL PALACE AT LA GRANJA DE
SAN ILDEFONSO

GREAT GALLERIES SERIES

THE ESCORIAL

THE ROYAL PALACE AT LA GRANJA DE
SAN ILDEFONSO

Text by
JUAN DE CONTRERAS Y LOPEZ DE AYALA
MARQUÉS DE LOZOYA

MEREDITH PRESS · NEW YORK

First published in the United States in 1967
by MEREDITH PRESS
Des Moines and New York

Translated from the Italian
by
James Brockway

Printed in Italy for Meredith Press

© Istituto Geografico De Agostini S.p.A. - Novara - 1965

THE ESCORIAL

It would not be strictly accurate to describe the monastery of San Lorenzo del Escorial as the most representative of all monuments in Spain, for it has very many different sides to its character, while some of its features have possibly found even more convincing expression in other architectural monuments. One would, however, venture to say that it is in this mighty edifice, erected by Philip II, that Spain's determination to remain European and to hold her own against the powerful influence of oriental civilizations, manifests itself in the most impressive fashion—a determination occasioned by the constant presence of the Orient and ever active beneath the surface. The Escorial is, besides, the most significant monument of the era of the Spanish Empire, when the Kings of Spain controlled Naples, Milan, Sicily, Sardinia, the Low Countries and Portugal and, with their overseas possessions in America, Africa and the South Seas, ruled over the greatest empire the world had seen. From early times onwards, the western world has been united by cultural trends which, time and again, spread out over the ' provinces ' from some particular centre which, for certain historical reasons, acquired the rank of a metropolis. In these cycles, the rôle Spain usually had to play was that of the ' provinces ', adopting the general rules which had been formulated elsewhere, in such metropolises as Rome or Constantinople, Baghdad, Florence or Paris, and adapting them to its own individual character. But in the reign of Philip II and his immediate successors, Spain performed the function of a capital itself, not so much for the rest of Europe but for the whole of the new world, and it did so with vigour and persistence. The Escorial is the architectural expression of that function.

Even though the Escorial is one of the most extraordinary buildings in Spain, all its various components come from beyond the country's frontiers. Anyone versed in the history of art will experience no difficulty in detecting how much the edifice owes to a Bramante, a Vignola, to the architecture of Flanders or of the Tyrol; and yet there can be few buildings in the world whose individual character is so pronounced and so unmistakable. Even though its different parts suggest origins in the most diverse corners of Europe, the Escorial could only have come into being in one country, in Spain, and at one moment in history, in the age of Philip II. It is the architectural expression of a cultural movement which reaches its zenith with Francisco Suárez in philosophy, Fray Luis de León in literature, El Greco in painting, and with Tomás Luis de Victoria in music. This movement might be defined as the endeavour to ' christen ' the Renaissance, to permeate it with the spirit of the Middle Ages, which lived on in the Spain of the religious struggles. In the Spanish peninsula, the Renaissance had not succeeded in pushing the Middle Ages to the outer limits, as it had in other countries. The medieval spirit lived on until well into the 18th century, with its wholehearted devotion to spiritual values and yearning for the Eternal, to the exclusion of the material considerations of life on earth.

A great historian, Father José de Sigüenza, was present to witness the building of the Escorial, and his account of the vicissitudes which accompanied its construction is among the finest pieces of Castilian prose. The plan to erect a monastery was twofold in origin—as clearly appears from the deed of foundation. On the one hand, Philip II wanted to fulfil his father's last wish. He, Charles of Spain (the Emperor Charles V of Germany), had wanted a pantheon to be built in which his mortal remains should lie side by side with those of his beloved wife, Isabella of Portugal. On the other hand, Philip II had vowed to erect a monastery and to dedicate this to St Laurence, on whose day, August 10th, in 1577, he had won his decisive victory over the French at St Quentin.

To provide regular and worthy services in this new house of God, which had also been conceived as the pantheon of the monarchs of Spain, the Spanish Order of St Jerome was selected, an Order which devoted itself primarily to the preservation of the beauty and splendour of the divine service and the observance of liturgical forms. The Emperor Charles V had already shown a marked preference for this Order, when, after his abdication, he retreated to the solitude of its monastery of Yuste. According to Philip II's conception, the Escorial was to become a great memorial church, a royal pantheon and a retreat. Here the Kings of Spain would be able to withdraw in order to meditate upon the eternal truths and to devote themselves to the tasks involved in ruling their giant empire. In fact, for its founder, the King-bureaucrat, who sought to concentrate all the affairs of his world-wide empire in his own hands, the monastery was a summer residence, as the palace at Medina Azahara had been to the Caliphs of Córdoba, and Versailles was to be to Louis XIV of France.

Always procrastinating, ever irresolute, Philip II was long in deciding upon a site for the enormous edifice he had planned. At one time he considered the high plateau of San Cristóbal in the vicinity of Segovia, later Manzanares el Real, and also Aranjuez. However, he finally decided on a slope on the south-east side of the Sierra de Guadarrama, which was thickly wooded and where there were many springs. This site, moreover, answered the requirements; it was not far from Madrid, only about 20 miles, yet far enough from the capital to guarantee the desired seclusion. The landscape was wild and mountainous, strewn with granite boulders, and in harmony with the austere nature of the King. Yet there were pleasant little copses, too, and dense forests, in those days teeming with game. Indeed, part of the peculiar charm of the Escorial lies in the perfect harmony between the building and its natural setting.

In the year 1562, Philip spent Holy Week in the nearby Hieronymite monastery of Guisando. On the way back to Madrid he broke his journey at El Escorial, spending the whole day there to explore the region and to take a good look at the landscape. Immediately after this, the work of clearing the site began. A few days later the King returned, bringing with him Juan Bautista de Toledo, a rather mysterious figure who, during a protracted stay in Italy, had won a good name for himself as an architect, mathematician and gifted draughtsman. It was he who designed the original plan.

On April 23, 1563 the first stone was laid in the presence of the King, Fray Juan de Huete, the prior-designate of the new monastic community, and several other personalities. Juan Bautista de Toledo directed the work of building the monastery until his death on May 21, 1567; his difficult task then passing to Juan de Herrera, who came from the Valle de Trasmiera, a mountain valley near Santander, a region which from time immemorial had given Spain her finest stone-masons. It is possible that Rodrigo Gil de Hontañón was called in too, to act as a consultant. He had been the architect for the cathedrals at Salamanca and Segovia, of the university at Alcalá de Henares and of the Palacio de Monterrey in Salamanca. Various designs for the church had been commissioned from Italy; that chosen being by Paciotto da Urbino and inspired by Bramante's plans for St Peter's in Rome. Herrera, however, made some changes in this design as the building proceeded.

Padre Sigüenza has left us a very lively account of the course the building operations followed. Close to the site an entire town came into being for the workers and their crafts, excellently managed by Fray Antonio de Villacastín, who was in charge of all technical matters. It was due to the latter's devotion and skill that the King's wishes were fulfilled. The stone-masons, carvers and bricklayers required to fit the ashlars together and to perform the essential bricklaying were innumerable. The most skilled woodworkers were assembled from every corner of Europe, from simple carpenters, whose skill still astounds architects today, to the leading cabinet-makers and wood-carvers of the time. It was exactty the same with the metal-workers. In the smithies enormous quantities of iron and steel parts were manufactured, and the most beautiful pieces cast in lead, bronze or copper in smelting furnaces which the craftsmen had built themselves. While it was under construction, the Escorial became a veritable school of the fine arts-painters, sculptors, goldsmiths, miniaturists, silversmiths, organbuilders and bell-founders who had come together there in scores.

It proved possible to lay the first stone on September 13, 1584, and the church was consecrated on August 9, 1586 on the eve of St Laurence's Day.

6

At the end of his life, the founder-monarch elected to spend the days of his long illness in the Escorial. He died there on September 13, 1598, in his own small chamber, from which he had been able to follow the masses celebrated at the high altar.

During his lifetime Philip II had been interested in the arts and sciences. In his unadorned apartments were many instruments used in physics and mathematics, maps, and a collection of splendid watercolour studies of animals by Albrecht Dürer. In addition to the rooms of the monastery and palace, there was a library, where in exceptionally beautiful surroundings Philip had sought to assemble a unique collection of costly books and manuscripts, and a museum, among the most exquisite in the world, containing masterpieces by Gerard David, Roger van der Weyden, Hieronymus Bosch, Joachim Patinier, Titian, Tintoretto, Veronese, El Greco, Sánchez Coello, Pantoja and many other great painters. The monastery's collection of vestments, manuscripts containing valuable miniatures, and of costly accessories used in the celebration of mass is still impressive today, despite losses due to war and fire.

Philip II's successor increased the riches already amassed by the monastery's founder. Philip III had the statues made by the Leonis for the royal family vault erected in the church and started work on the construction of the pantheon for the monarchs of Spain. He enriched the church's collections with countless costly items and the library with more than three thousand Arabic manuscripts from the library of Muley Zidan, the Sultan of Morocco. Philip IV completed the pantheon. He was a passionate art collector and acquired paintings for the museum by Velázquez, Ribera and other great masters. Charles II had the good fortune that had been denied to Philip II—in Luca Giordano he finally found a decorator of genius for the Escorial. The Italian artist's frescoes, in the arches of the church and above the main staircase of the monastery, are among the noblest achievements of Baroque painting in Europe. It was Charles II who founded the Altar of the Holy Host in the sacristy, whose baroque forms frame the last masterpiece of the Spanish school—a magnificent work by Claudio Coello.

The first Bourbons among the kings of Spain—Philip V and Louis I, both of whose reigns were brief, and Ferdinand VI—could not be charmed by the Escorial. The monastery and the pantheon were too gloomy to suit their taste, striking too sharp a contrast with the spirit of the times. It was not until the reign of Charles III (1759-1788) that an academic preference for the severe classical style brought the building into favour once again. The finest Spanish architect of the time, Juan de Villanueva, was fundamentally a posthumous pupil of Herrera's. For the monarch and his son, later Charles IV, both enthusiastic huntsmen, the woods in the neighbourhood of the monastery were a veritable paradise—which will explain the frequency of the court's sojourns in the Escorial. The royal apartments in the palace were embellished and sumptuously decorated according to the taste of the day, while in order to meet the essential requirements of the complicated bureaucracy of the Bourbons, subsidiary buildings were also erected in the same style as the monastery. Under Juan de Villanueva's direction, two delightful small pleasure palaces were erected, the Prince's Pavilion and the Upper Pavilion, or Infante's Pavilion. Charles IV turned the palace into a museum of furniture and tapestries and Goya, too, now joined the ranks of the great artists whose names add lustre to the Escorial's history. Finally, Ferdinand VII expended enormous sums on repairing the damage done by Napoleon's troops, and Isabella II had the Pantheon of the Infantes built —at great expense but with little taste.

What surprises one most about the Escorial—a building it had taken many years and many different architects to complete—is its wonderful unity. Its architecture betrays nothing of the twists and turns of policy which the documents record. This unity can doubtless be traced to the personality of the founder. Philip II was not merely proficient in mathematics and architecture—several architectural designs are attributed to him—but he was also a precise and pedantic man, obsessed by an exaggerated sense of responsibility, which caused him to concern himself with every small detail of the building. The 'pharaohic' concept of the monument, which was preserved despite the succession of divergent architects who had charge of the building operations, was due to him. Everything was to be subordinated to reason, nothing was to be left to the imagination. The aim was to arrive at the highest form of beauty, which does not come from ornamentation (lacking here in any case) but from order, proportion and harmony in the design, and from the quality and perfect treatment of materials. The Escorial is pure architecture — no concession to decoration will be found here. The preference was for the Doric style, which restricts the architect to working with set-square and compasses with no resort at all to assistance from the sculptor. Everything is lucid and logical—like the theology of the Council of Trent. Nothing superfluous or useless is tolerated. Each component serves an absolutely definite purpose. As a result, the beauty of the Escorial depends solely on the simple clarity of a mathematical equation.

This strict adherence to a consciously chosen method also explains the many different verdicts on the building which have been arrived at through the centuries. For Philip II's contemporaries, the Escorial was the eighth wonder of the world, and for the space of a century the architects of Spain and of the Spanish overseas territories could think of nothing better to do than to emulate this example, which had become the outward expression of Spain's world domination. Even in the exaggerated Baroque of a José de Churriguera, the underlying structure has still been influenced by the Escorial, even if it is covered with thick foliage. The rejection of the Spanish way of thought which made itself felt among intellectuals and minorities at the court during the reign of the first Bourbons, caused the Escorial to lose prestige in favour of the academic Baroque style which remained dominant in the rest of Europe. It was the architects of Charles III who were to take Philip II's creation as their guide once again in their effort to arrive at a more sober and severe classicism. Juan de Villanueva, the most famous of them, had learned a great deal from Herrera. 19th century romanticism, on the other hand, naturally rejected a building which made no concessions at all to the imagination. To the romantics of this time the Escorial was the image, in stone, of Philip II's mind, which, in the short novel *Don Carlos* by the Abbé de Saint-Réal (1639-1692) and Schiller's play of the same title, had been portrayed to all Europe as the very incarnation of fanaticism, hypocrisy and cruelty. One romantic poet, José Manuel Quintana (1772-1857), went so far indeed as to describe Philip as " the earthly patron of the infamous in art and in men ".

Romantic sensibility continued to be operative in Europe until the turn of the century. Men searched in medieval ruins, in Moorish architecture, in the old towns, for what the Escorial could not offer: namely the picturesque. In our own day, when the preference is for a pure and functional architecture devoid of all ornamentation, architects have discovered a forerunner in Juan de Herrera, and once again the Escorial is seen as the eighth wonder of the world, as it was in the days of its royal founder. Poets and critics have rediscovered its hidden poetic vein; the suppressed passion which is latent there, beneath an apparently cool, geometrical surface. Here is the verdict of a writer of our own day, the poet and architect Luis Felipe Vivanco Bergamín (b. 1907) on Herrera's work:

" It was the new conception of architecture which Herrera introduced in the self-contradictory spirit of the Spanish Renaissance that first made the brilliant development of our Baroque architecture possible. At last the Spanish genius had acquired a place of its own, materially as well as spiritually, where it could develop freely. Those who see the Escorial as a genuinely Spanish product, despite the Italian influence apparent in its form, are therefore right. For it is really not yet a matter of form —as it was later on with Baroque (in this field Herrera is a purist and would definitely not have adapted himself)—it is a matter of the arrangement and appraisal of both inner and outer volumes, or, if one insists on speaking of form, then of ' spatial form '. An artist who goes to work intuitively is never concerned with the final result. But Herrera was not a spontaneous artist; he belonged to a far greater extent to those artists who are concerned with the end-results, in that they make intelligent use of all the possibilities already at hand."

This is a very Spanish attitude. One does not encounter the gift of creative originality very often in Spain, but one does find the ability to mould and develop trends reaching the country from other parts, and, indeed, to achieve the most astonishing results with these. This is true, for example, of Velázquez, who made the most of the stimulus he received from the Venetians and from Michelangelo and Caravaggio.

The royal palace occupies about a quarter of the chequered ground plan of the building, the north-east corner, that is, ignoring the church. The projection at the front, on the east-west axis, the handle to the giant grid which the Escorial's plan represents (a reminder of the martyrdom which its patron saint suffered), also forms part of the palace. Its rooms are grouped around one large and two small interior courtyards. It is the least pretentious residence the Hapsburgs and Bourbons ever occupied. The most striking apartments are those of Philip II, which have been left as good as unaltered, in memory of the building's founder. Their cell-like austerity, seen against the most refined luxury elsewhere, is very moving. These are small, humble rooms, white-washed and lacking in all decoration but for the blue wall-tiles from Talavera. It was from these rooms that Philip II ruled over the greatest empire the world had seen 'since Adam's day'. But this austerity was to the monarch's taste. Of him Padre Francisco de los Santos writes: ' He did not seem to come here as a king but as one of the severest of monks'. The few beautiful pieces of furniture and the valuable pictures which enliven these rooms are in visible contrast to this sobriety. Yet the only apartment of truly palatial dimensions is the Hall of Battles, a gallery, on the walls of which frescoes by Italian artists depict episodes from the Reconquista, the Battle of Higueruela, and scenes — relating to Philip's own time — from the war with France and the campaign against Portugal. The apartments used by later kings are suites of long, simple rooms, devoid of all architectural display. At the time of the Hapsburgs, the only decoration in these rooms was the same as that found in Philip II's apartments — the blue tiles of Talavera. Yet when the Court stayed there, the ' billeting officer ', following the custom in the royal castles, conferred a certain splendour on these rooms by covering the floors and walls with carpets and tapestries. Charles IV, a Bourbon, was the first to attempt to enliven and embellish the palace's all too sombre apartments a little. He was fortunate in having one of the greatest of all the Spanish architects, Juan de Villanueva (1739-1811), to direct the operations, a man who owed his experience above all to his employment on this great work of Juan de Herrera's. Today the palace apartments are worth seeing on account of the marvellous collection of tapestries they contain, a large part of which were manufactured in the royal tapestry factory at Madrid to designs by court painters such as Bayeu, Castillo and, first and foremost, Goya. The colours in these tapestries were of a splendour hitherto unknown in the art of weaving pictures. Like all the royal residences in Spain, the Escorial palace, too, is rich in beautiful pieces of furniture and valuable items of porcelain. Some of the panelling, in precious woods, shows the degree of perfection reached by the craftsmen working at the court of Charles IV.

THE PRINCE'S PAVILION AND THE INFANTE'S PAVILION. In all the royal residences in the neighbourhood of Madrid one finds small pavilions amid gardens, a little removed from the palace itself. These were not actually lived in, but were designed to provide the princes with a place where they could spend a few hours of relaxation with their friends. All over Europe in the 18th century, a need was felt to flee the splendid, but not particularly comfortable, salons of the enormous, baroque palaces of the day and to withdraw to the more intimate atmosphere of small rooms. Neither of the pavilions at the Escorial are really inhabitable as is le Petit Trianon; their aim is rather to create the carefree atmosphere of country life, like Le Hameau de la Reine at Versailles. Actually, they have taken the small casinos found at country seats in Italy as their model, and it is significant that they should have been introduced at the court of Spain when Maria Luisa of Parma was Queen.

The small rooms in these pavilions are crammed with the most exquisite paintings and sculptures, works of art in porcelain, bronze and ivory; yet all harmonizing with the elegant proportions of these sumptuous toys.

Both of the Escorial pavilions were built by Juan de Villanueva in 1772, the Lower Pavilion for the Prince of Asturias, later Charles IV, and the Upper Pavilion for his brother, the Infante Gabriel. Juan de Villanueva is the Spanish representative of the severe neo-classicism of the later 18th century which was mitigated by an early romantic strain. In his genre, de Villanueva perhaps even surpasses Schinkel. The Prince's Pavilion and its garden combine to make one of the most enchanting spots in the surroundings of Madrid. It bears the most eloquent witness to a court of the early Romantic period which was to see the decline and later the fall of the Spanish Empire; yet on which a select band — Goya, Villanueva, Jovellanos, Moratín, Meléndez Valdés — conferred an atmosphere, of great distinction and culture. Its salons are tiny yet splendid museums, designed to house numerous small gems. The Upper Pavilion, more supple and graceful of line, with a wonderful view across the splendid landscape in the vicinity, gives the impression of being a kind of hunting lodge. Yet it served for the musical performances organized by the Infante Gabriel, who was the most cultured and intelligent of Charles III's sons and a great connoisseur of fine books and good music. In the rotunda, in the heart of the pavilion, those few among the courtiers who preferred Bach or Mozart to the popular airs of the day would gather together around the Abbé Soler.

Spain is the country of violent contrasts. One ought, therefore, to speak about it in the plural, not merely to indicate the diversity of parts which went to make up the ancient monarchy, but to point also to the simultaneous existence of different, indeed, diametrically opposed Spains at every period of the country's history. To all appearances, there is no greater contrast than that between the bare expanses of the Escorial Church or the austerity of Philip II's apartments, and the apartments occupied by the Bourbons with their rich tapestries designed by Goya, or the salons in the Prince's Pavilion. Yet there is a spiritual bond linking all the Escorial's divergent parts, and this is the desire of a minority in Spain, a desire persisting throughout the centuries, to join up with the great cultural movements of Europe while preserving a specifically Spanish character.

San Lorenzo del Escorial

On April 23, 1563 the first stone was laid of what was to become a gigantic complex of buildings—a church, a royal pantheon, a monastery and a palace—all of which can be seen on the photograph overleaf. The architect in charge was Juan Bautista de Toledo, who had won great renown in Italy and who was appointed architect-royal on August 12, 1561. It is possible that Juan Bautista de Toledo had known the great Italian architects of his day and had brought back with him from Italy drawings and designs by Palladio and Vignola. Until his death on May 19, 1567, Toledo enjoyed Philip II's full confidence. Although the original design underwent many modifications as the work of building progressed, by and large Toledo's plan was adhered to, as Padre José de Sigüenza assures us in his history of the building of this great edifice. The famous architect Juan de Herrera was already working with Juan Bautista de Toledo in 1563 and it was he who was to confer on the Escorial its definitive form.

The symmetry of the first design was of particular interest. Only the great dome was to interrupt the play of lines of the huge rectangular façades.

Aerial View (pages 12-13) ▶

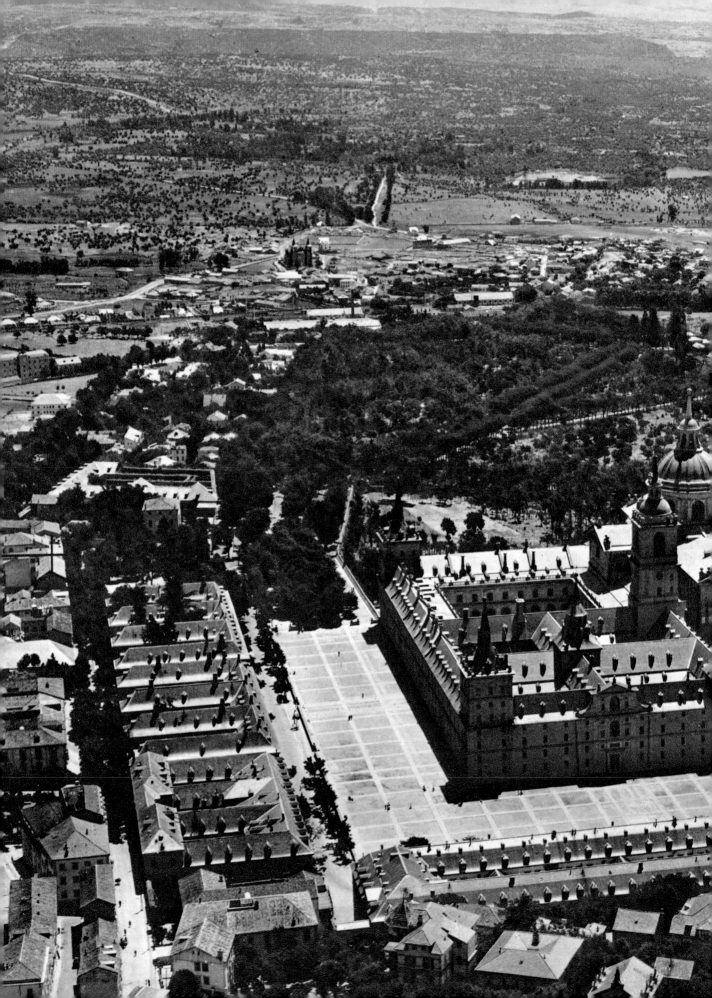

The Escorial – View across the Roofs

Although the Renaissance set its stamp on the overall design, the Escorial also has one pronouncedly Spanish feature—the chequered or tessellated ground-plan. This divides up the enormous surface area covered by the building into so many different blocks, in which the apartments are grouped, as in Moorish palaces, around interior courtyards. This was in line with Spanish taste, which, influenced by the East, avoids vast open spaces. Another reminder of the Middle Ages is afforded by the square towers at the four corners, which give the building the appearance of a castle, an Alcázar. Indicative of the expansion of the Habsburg Empire are the steeply sloping roofs of slates and the attractive spires with which the towers are crowned. They derive from central Europe, from Southern Germany, the Tyrol, and from Flanders.

The Dome (see also plate on p. 19) ▶

This is without doubt one of the most beautiful cupolas built in Europe during the Renaissance. It is not known whether it formed part of the original design by Juan Bautista de Toledo or whether it derives from the designs which Paciotto, the Italian engineer and architect, had supplied from Urbino, based on Bramante's original design for St Peter's at Rome. The architect Lorente Juntera states that the earliest example is the dome of Santa Maria de Carignano in Genoa.

Galería de Convalecientes

The *Galería de Convalecientes* (Convalescents' Gallery) in the south 'cheerful' side of the Escorial. The two-storeyed gallery was given this name, since, being close to the hospital section and protected from the north wind, it was used by older and ailing monks for short walks. For a long time the design was attributed to Francisco de Mora, who died in 1611. Today, however, it seems certain that Juan Bautista de Toledo designed the gallery. Arches alternate with architraves, resting on Doric columns arranged in pairs, in the style of the Italian architect, Palladio. Along the upper storey, slender Ionic columns support a single architrave.

The south façade, with this gallery reflected in a pool designed by Francisco de Mora, is undoubtedly the friendliest of the Escorial's façades. There is a magnificent view across the Castilian plain from the garden, which, laid out in rectangles planted with box, echoes the geometrical design of the monastery.

Spire of Escorial Tower ▶

The appropriate form for the spires of the towers was found in a charming play of surfaces. The carpentry bears witness to the same striving for perfection that characterizes the rest of the building.

The South Front

The basic ideas underlying Juan de Herrera's design are perfectly evident from this view of the south front, even if Philip II did keep a close watch on the building operations and often introduced changes of his own. Like the pyramids of Egypt, this grandiose edifice disdains all ornament. Everything is geometry in the Escorial, the beauty of the building depending solely on the precisely calculated proportions of its several parts, on the quality of the reddish granite used and careful craftsmanship.

In front of this huge complex of buildings lies a large terrace. This terrace rests on a vault about 26 feet high and 1,800 feet long, the façade is composed of 77 rounded arches. The garden has been laid out with box-trees grouped round twelve fountains above this vault, its present design going back to the 18th century. According to Padre Sigüenza, at the time of the monastery's foundation the garden was planted with a mass of multicoloured flowers in the oriental manner.

The Dome (see also plate on p. 15) ▶

The dome of the Escorial church rests on a square socle, from each corner of which a flight of steps appears. The arches and pillars (Doric half-columns) of the cylindrical tambour are reminiscent of the church of Santa Maria di Carignano in Genoa.

The Main Entrance Front

This appears to be wholly the work of Juan de Herrera. A start was made with its construction in 1576. The centre block, containing the main entrance, is two storeys higher than the rest of the building. According to Camón Aznar, ' the façade of the monastery is of outstanding significance in the history of Spanish art, for it is here that the baroque conception of form makes its entry into our architecture.' To this well-known art historian, the unique feature is the limited emphasis that has been laid on the main doorway. While in Renaissance churches and cathedrals this was often given the dimensions of a triumphal arch, here it seems as though it has been tucked away in the mass of masonry. The portal consists of two sets of bold columns, the one set above the other. The lower façade is divided up by niches and windows in the manner of Palladio.

◀ *The Church*

The church, which Juan de Herrera built on the basis of the plans Paciotto sent from Urbino, is purely Italianate and has no prototype in Spain. The ground plan is based on a Greek cross above the intersection of which rises the dome, supported by a substructure devoid of all ornamentation.

Front Façade of the Church

The main entrance to the church is at the far end of the Courtyard of the Kings. This façade was probably designed by Paciotto and built by Juan de Herrera. According to Paciotto's design, the towers must have been completed before 1570. The other sections and the façade were executed under Juan de Herrera's supervision.

IOSAPHAT   EZECHIAS

The Statues of the Kings

The Courtyard of the Kings derives its name from the six huge statues of the Old Testament kings connected with the building of the temple at Jerusalem. They were hewn from granite by Juan Bautista Monegro, known as de Toledo, the heads having been executed in marble. The bronze, fire-gilded crowns, sceptres and other insignia are the work of the sculptor Sebastián Fernández.

The Courtyard of the Evangelists

The Courtyard of the Evangelists, the main cloisters in the monastery, is beyond question the finest architectural work to be seen and admired in the Escorial. It is wholly the work of Juan Bautista de Toledo. The arcades—inspired, according to Camón Aznar, by the Colosseum—and the small temple in the centre reveal Toledo's training in Rome.

The Monks' Choir

It was the intention that the Escorial's severe architectural lines should be balanced by the use of the brightest possible colours in the frescoes adorning the vaults, but Philip II was not fortunate in the choice of his painter. After vain efforts to commission Veronese to do this work, Luca Cambiaso, a Genoese artist, was called on to paint the frescoes on the vaults above the main chapel and the Monks' Choir. Above the choir he painted a *Gloria*, a paltry, mannered composition in garish colours. The choir stalls, with their beautiful Corinthian-style decoration, two rows on either side, were designed by Juan de Herrera and carved out of costly woods by Giuseppe Flecha, an Italian, and the Spanish craftsmen, Gamboa, Quesada, Serrano and Aguirre. Gil Brevot was commissioned to build the two organs, being considered at the time the finest organ builder in all Europe. The frescoes on the walls depict scenes from the life of St Laurence and are the work of the Florentine artist, Romolo Cincinnato.

The Intersection of the Nave

According to Camón Aznar, the design of the central section of the church determined the design of the whole. Paciotto made much use of Michelangelo's method of laying great stress on massive pillars.

The Frescoes in the Vaults of the Church

Charles II, the last of the Hapsburgs to sit on the throne of Spain, commissioned the Neapolitan artist, Luca Giordano, known as 'Fapresto', to do this work. He was, without doubt, the most outstanding decorative painter of the later 17th century.

The Statue of St Peter

It was due solely to Philip II that the Escorial has acquired such great historical and artistic significance. For example, as Duke of Milan, he was in a position to ensure that the architecture of a man of Juan de Herrera's calibre was enhanced by the splendid and highly fastidious sculpture produced by the Leoni workshop in Milan, a studio which had already served his father, Charles V. It was on January 10, 1579 that Pompeo Leoni signed the contract for the supply of the statues of the saints and the groups of sculpture designed to adorn the immense triptych, consisting of the high altar and the two royal tombs, in the main chapel. He was assisted in this work by a number of compatriots, Giacomo da Trezzo (known, in Spain, as Jacome Trezo), Giambattista Comane and Pietro Castello. Pompeo Leoni had to go to Milan for five years in 1582 in connection with the casting. It is quite probably that his father, Leone Leoni, then an old man, made the moulds and supervised the casting processes.

The Statue of St Paul

The bronze statues in the Escorial represent the finest works of Italian sculpture in the period between Michelangelo and Bernini. The elegant and majestic attitudes of the apostles, the perfect modelling of the faces, hands and robes, the impression of quiet strength the figures give—all this makes of each of them an exquisite work of art. The flawless casting, sensitive chasing and gilding have played their rôle, too, in achieving this result — crafts which in Milan in the late 16th century were practised with a perfection never equalled since.

The High Altar (page 30) ▶

Juan de Herrera, who had gradually become the architect-dictator of the Escorial, also made the architectural designs for the reredos. It was executed in marble and jasper by the sculptor Giacomo da Trezzo. The base and capital of the columns are made of bronze and were fashioned in the Leoni workshop in Milan. The paintings in the first section are the work of Pellegrino Tibaldi, those in the second and third are by Federico Zuccari. The Leonis made the twelve statues of the Apostles and the three exceptionally beautiful Calvary figures. The reredos is about 85 feet high and 45 feet wide.

The House of the Sacrament ▶

The House of the Sacrament was designed by Juan de Herrera and built by Giacomo da Trezzo. On a jasper socle stand eight columns of blood-red jasper with Corinthian capitals in bronze supporting a circular cornice. This in its turn supports a further socle, cylindrical in shape and spanned by the dome. On twelve pedestals arranged round the socle stand bronze statues of the twelve apostles.

The Tomb of the emperor Charles V

The tombs of Charles V and of his son Philip II, which lie on either side of the high altar in the Escorial church, are among the most solemn and beautiful in all Europe. They are the work of Juan de Herrera and Pompeo Leoni. Both groups are reminiscent of the bronze statues which surround the tomb of the Emperor Maximilian at Innsbruck.

The Escutcheon above the Tomb of the Emperor Charles V

Tomb of Philip II ▶

Princess Maria of Portugal, first wife of Philip II, and her son, Don Carlos (page 35) ▶

The Escutcheon above the Tomb of Philip II

Luca Cambiaso *(Moneglia near Genoa, 1527 - El Escorial, 1585): The Gloria.
Fresco above the choir in the Escorial Church* ▶

LUCA GIORDANO (Naples, 1632-1705): Frescoes in (top) the Vaults of the Church and (above) the Main Staircase of the Monastery

On August 31, 1692 Charles II commissioned the painter Luca Giordano, known in Spain as Lucas Jordán, to paint the vault over the main stair in the Escorial monastery. Giordano worked until April 1693, creating one of the most significant works of decorative painting in Europe. The frieze, a detail of which is shown in the lower illustration, depicts the Battle of St Quentin.

The upper illustration shows the fresco in the third main vault of the church ceiling. In the centre one sees Moses receiving the Commandments from Jehovah. At the sides many other Old Testament scenes are depicted containing many splendidly painted figures. In one of the lunettes we see Bezaleel and Aholiab, ' wise in all manner of workmanship ', who built the ' Ark of the Covenant ' and the ' altar of burnt offering ' (Exodus, 31). According to the letters the prior wrote to Charles II, Giordano worked at this fresco in 1694.

The Monks' Choir

The lofty Monks' Choir rests on an almost flat vault constructed of squared blocks of granite, a further indication of Juan de Herrera's wide knowledge of the art of working in stone and the opportunities afforded by this medium. Herrera had a stone and bronze lectern, weighing several tons, placed immediately above the vertex of the vault. This lectern consists of a square socle of red jasper with inlaid stripes in white marble, supporting four rectangular columns of gilded bronze. Between them there is a contrivance with the aid of which the heavy lectern, 35 ft all round, can be turned without difficulty. Above there is a small temple of marble and precious woods containing an effigy of the Virgin Mary.

BENVENUTO CELLINI *(Florence, 1500-1571):   The Marble Christ* ▶

One of the most famous works of art in the Escorial is Benvenuto Cellini's Crucifixion, in Carrara marble—(see detail of head on p. 43). It hangs in a small chapel behind the choir of the church, so that on certain occasions it can be seen from the Courtyard of the Kings.

39

Entrance to the Pantheon of the Kings

Under the royal coat of arms in the magnificent marble and bronze entrance to the pantheon, there is an inscription in Latin the last section of which reads: 'Philip IV, great in mercy, constancy and piety, enlarged, embellished and completed it in the year of the Lord 1654'.

The Pantheon of the Kings

Giovanni Battista Crescenzi designed the pantheon in the form of a sixteen-sided polygon. The marble and bronze sarcophagi contain the mortal remains of the Spanish kings, both Hapsburgs and Bourbons, from Charles I (The Emperor Charles V) to Alphonso XII, with the exception of Philip V, whose remains lie at San Ildefonso, and Ferdinand VI, whose grave is in Madrid.

DOMENICO GUIDI *(Torano, near Carrara, 1625 - Rome, 1701)*: *Crucifix in the Pantheon of the Kings*

Palomino, the chronicler, reports that in 1659 a bronze crucifix was brought to Spain, which crucifix the Duke of Terranova had had made for Philip IV by ' a nephew of Giuliano Finelli ', a pupil of Algardi's. According to Elías Tormo the nephew of Giuliano Finelli must have been Domenico Guidi, the sculptor.

Entrance to the Pantheon of the Infantes

In 1862 Isabella II gave her approval to the designs which José Segundo de Lema, her architect-royal, had drawn up for a large pantheon. It was intended to provide a last resting-place for queens whose children did not become rulers, for the Infantes of Spain and for foreign princes related to the Spanish royal house. The building was completed in 1888.

The Tomb of Don John of Austria

Don John of Austria (1547-1578), a natural son of the Emperor Charles V, was a great general. He defeated the Moors near Granada, the rebels in the Low Countries, and the Turks in the great naval battle off Lepanto. He died in the Belgian city of Namur, his remains finally reaching the Escorial by a remarkably devious route. Isabella II had him laid to rest in one of the rooms of the Pantheon of the Infantes. His tomb was designed by Ponciano Ponzano y Gascón and executed in Carrara marble by the Italian sculptor Giuseppe Galeotti.

Ponciano Ponzano y Gascón (1813-1877) was the leading Spanish sculptor of the era of romantic Neo-classicism. He had worked in Rome with Horace Vernet, with Thorwaldsen and with Tenerani. Some of his works met with great success and were reproduced by the engraver Salvatore Betti.

46

The Sacristy

The sacristy is a long, rectangular room, 330 feet in length and about 26 feet broad and high. The ceiling, a flattened barrel vault with lunettes, was painted with grotesques in the style of Raphael by Fabrizio Castello and Niccolò Granello, sons of Giambattista Castello, known as 'El Bergamesco'. The entire western wall of the sacristy is occupied by a line of chests of drawers carved from precious woods, in which the vestments vessels and paraments used during the celebration of Mass are kept. Above these, along the wall, runs a line of small Corinthian columns. The large mirror in the centre, framed in silver and decorated with rock crystal, was a gift from Marianne of Austria, wife of Philip IV. At the far end one can see the Altar of the Holy Host, founded by Charles II and containing the celebrated painting of Claudio Coello. The sacristy also contains some very fine oil-paintings by Titian and Jusepe de Ribera.

CLAUDIO COELLO (*Madrid, c. 1635-1693*): *The Adoration of the Holy Host by Charles II—in the Sacristy* ▶

This painting contains a wealth of excellent portraits—of the King, the prior, Fray Francisco de los Santos, the Dukes of Alba, Medinaceli, Pastrana and other historical figures besides the painter.

47

16th Century Vestments and Paraments used at Mass

The Altar of the Holy Host in the Sacristy ▶

This altar was built by order of Charles II according to designs by José del Olmo, the architect-royal, and is made of jasper, marble and gilded bronze. In it the host profaned by the Dutch Protestants in 1572 was reputed to be kept. The crucifix, of gilded bronze, is the work of Pietro Tacca, and the decorations, likewise of bronze, are by Francesco Filippini. The altar was consecrated in the year 1690.

EN MAGNI OPERIS MIRACVLVM
INTRA MIRACVLVM MVNDI
CŒLI MIRACVLÓ CONSECRATVM

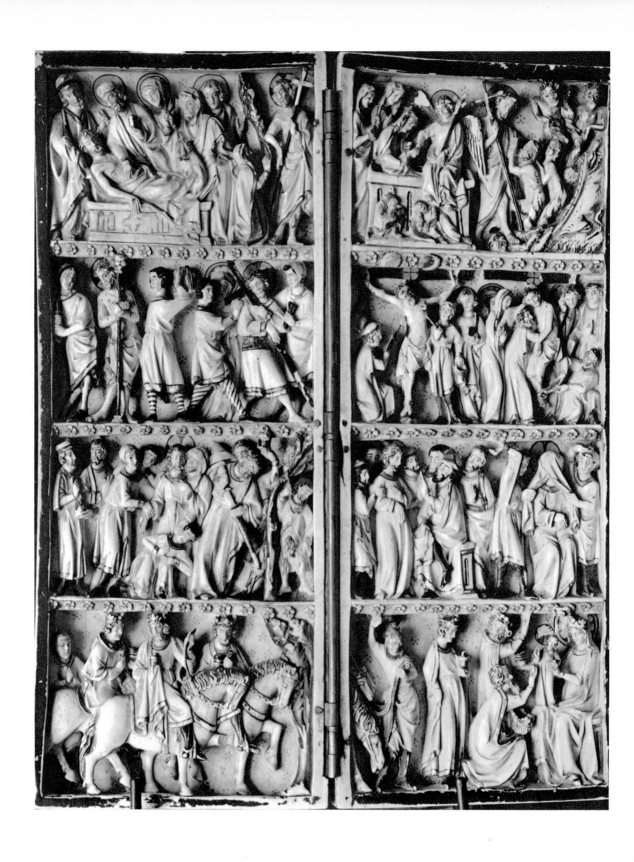

The Ivory Diptych (French, 14th century)

Detail of coloured Ivory Diptych

The prior's cell which adjoins the chapter-house is a museum containing many small treasures from the most diverse lands and ages; an enamelled copper casket from Limoges, 13th century work, a Mexican mitre constructed of feathers and dating back to the 16th century, the field altar of gilded silver used by the Emperor Charles V, and many other objects of silver and ivory. One of the most interesting pieces is a diptych consisting of ivory reliefs which have been coloured very delicately with gold and other colours, French in origin and dating back to the middle years of the 14th century (see plate opposite and detail above). The small figures, arranged in eight panels, depict scenes from the Gospels. Moving from the bottom onwards these are: The Journey and Adoration of the Magi, The Taking of Christ in the Garden of Gethsemane, Christ before Pilate, The Mocking of Christ, The Flagellation, The Road to Golgotha and the Crucifixion, The Descent from the Cross, The Interment, The Resurrection, and Descent into Hell.

DOMENIKOS THEOTOKÓPULOS, known as EL GRECO *(Phodele near Candia on Crete, 1541 - Toledo, 1614):*
The Martyrdom of St. Maurice

The painting depicts the conference between the Captain-martyr and his associates, about the preparation for the martyrdom. Today this work is regarded as a masterpiece in the history of painting (detail opposite).

EL GRECO: *St. Peter – in the Sacristy* ▶

DIEGO RODRIGUEZ DE SILVA Y VELÁZQUEZ *(Seville, 1599 - Madrid, 1660)*: *The Sons of Jacob, showing their Father their Brother Joseph's Blood-stained Coat – in the Escorial Museum*

Although Velázquez had a great influence on the acquisition of paintings for the Escorial, the monastery contains only one of his own works. In August 1629 Velásquez, already enjoying the good-will of Philip IV, went on a trip to Italy. He went to Venice, Ferrara and Rome and stayed a year in order to copy paintings by Raphael and Michelangelo. Study of the great Italian painters strengthened his own work. This is already clearly evident in the two large oil paintings which he painted in Rome and which are very similar as regards their style of representation. He took these works back to Spain with him. One was *Vulcan's Forge*, the other the work reproduced here.

◀ EL GRECO: *The Adoration of the Name of Jesus – in the Sacristy*

This painting is one of El Greco's great masterpieces—one of the great masterpieces of all painting in fact. It is an artist's interpretation of a sentence from Paul's epistle to the Philippians: ' That at the name of Jesus every knee should bow, of things in heaven, and things in earth, and things under the earth.' (Phil. 2, 10). Among the angels and saints in the jaws of hell, Philip II can be seen.

JUSEPE DE RIBERA known as LO SPAGNOLETTO *(Jativa, 1590/91-Posillipo, 1652)*: *Jacob guarding Laban's Flock – in the Escorial Museum*

During his two journeys to Italy, Velázquez acquired Jusepe de Ribera's masterpieces for the royal palace in Madrid — today they can be found in the Prado Museum. Today it is only in Naples and in the royal galleries in Spain that it is possible to acquire an impression of the art of this brilliant painter. Ribera enriched the dark realism of the school of Caravaggio, so sympathetic to Spanish painters, with the wonderful luminosity of his Levantine palette. His sure draughtsmanship, the beauty of his composition, his mastery in depicting the precise nature of things on canvas, make Ribera one of the great masters of baroque painting. In the sacristy and in the chapter halls there was until a short time ago a considerable collection of Lo Spagnoletto's paintings, the most important of which are now on exhibition in the Escorial Museum.

PAOLO CALIARI known as VERONESE (*Verona, 1528 - Venice, 1588*): *The Annunciation – in the Escorial Museum*

The preference shown by Charles V and Philip II for the Venetian painters, and the fact that Velázquez, too, showed them a preference when purchasing paintings, have resulted in the Escorial possessing a significant collection of Venetian paintings.

Jacopo Robusti, *known as* Tintoretto *(Venice, 1518-1594):* *Mary Magdalene at Christ's Feet – in the Escorial Museum*

Tintoretto's painting showing Mary Magdalene washing Christ's feet is a splendid picture, exceptionally successful in its creation of atmosphere. There is a direct connection with the great oil painting of *The Preparation of the Lord's Supper*, which now hangs in the Prado in Madrid.

◀ Tiziano Vecellio, *known as* Titian *(Pieve di Cadore, c. 1489 - Venice, 1576):* *Crucifixion—in the Sacristy at the Escorial*

According to Wilhem Suida, this *Crucifixion*, one of Titian's most beautiful paintings, was painted between 1550 and 1560.

TITIAN: *The Last Supper – in the Escorial Museum*

The Last Supper is possibly the most important religious picture that Titian painted for Philip II. He worked on it for seven years, completing it in 1564. Unfortunately, despite the protests of the Spanish painter Juan Navarret, known as 'the Dumb', this splendid painting has been cut down

on each side, since it proved too big for the place accorded to it in the Refectory. There is a reproduction of the entire painting, though on a smaller scale, in the Brera Gallery in Milan. In his composition Titian was less influenced by Leonardo da Vinci's famous *Last Supper* than by an engraving made by the Italian engraver, Marcantonio, of a painting by Raphael.

HIERONYMUS VAN AKEN, *known as* HIERONYMUS BOSCH *(Hertogenbosch, 1450-1516):* *The Mocking of Christ, panel*

ROGIER VAN DER WEYDEN *(Tournai, c. 1400 - Brussels, 1464): Christ on the Cross between Mary and John* ▶

In painting the *Descent from the Cross*, in the Prado in Madrid, and this great painting in the Escorial, the famous painter of Tournai abandoned his favourite technique, miniature painting, to paint lifesize figures. Set against the red background, the three figures are as though hewn from stone. The painting originally hung in the palace at Valsain, near Segovia.

The Main Staircase in the Escorial

The great staircase of granite, which links the lower galleries of the cloisters, or Courtyard of the Evangelists, with the upper walks, was designed by Giambattista Castello, known as ' El Bergamesco '. The panels under the five large arches are the work of the Genoese artist, Luca (Luqueto) Cambiaso.

Luca Giordano: *Fresco on the Vault above the Main Staircase*

This fresco, completed in 1693, is one of the most important works of Baroque decorative painting. On three sides of the frieze there are paintings of the Battle of St Quentin, on the fourth a picture of the founding of the Escorial. The vault itself has been decorated with a *Gloria*.

The Hall of Battles in the Royal Palace

In 1587 Philip II commissioned the painters Niccolò Granello, Lazzaro Tavarone and Fabrizio Castello to decorate the 60 yard long wall of the palace gallery with a depiction of the Battle on the Higueruela, at which John II had defeated the Moors on July 1, 1431. Orazio Cambiaso, a son of Luqueto's, later joined this team. The requisite knowledge of detail was obtained from a large tapestry, *en grisaille*, dating from the 15th century. Probably a work of Nicolás Francés, this had been found in a chest in the Alcázar in Segovia. The painting covers the entire south wall of the gallery and represents a valuable document which enables us to picture this episode in the Reconquista (see detail left). On the wall opposite feats of arms of Philip II's time have been depicted: various episodes from the campaign against Henry II of France, the war with Portugal and scenes of the naval battles off the Azores. Rodrigo de Holanda drew the sketches for these frescoes. The same artist decorated the vaulted ceiling, taking as his example Raphael's decoration of the loggias in the Vatican.

Throne-Room in the Royal Palace

If we disregard the church, the apartments intended as a royal residence occupy about one quarter of the entire complex of the Escorial. They are contained within one half of the north and one half of the east front. Most of the palace's apartments were furnished and decorated during the reigns of the Bourbon kings, Charles III and Charles IV, and are characterized, like the other Bourbon palaces in the neighbourhood of Madrid, by a notable collection of tapestries, paintings and furniture dating from the second half of the 18th century. Fortunately, the rooms in the Escorial in which Philip II lived and died have been left virtually as they were. An attempt has been made to bring together furniture and paintings in these rooms which are in keeping with the taste and style of living of the Escorial's founder. In these not very spacious apartments, with their whitewashed walls decorated with Talavera tiles, one senses a remarkable contrast between monastic austerity and exquisite luxury. Here the bureaucratic monarch pined away, ruling over his huge empire with a painstaking attention to detail. The furnishing of the large throne-room, with its flattened barrel-vault ceiling, is exceedingly simple. The paintings and maps which adorn its walls are of no great interest. The Flemish tapestry under the canopy behind Charles V's throne is, however, a magnificent piece of work. So, too, are the tapestries on the wall on either side of the throne. They form part of the *Spheres Series* and are among the most beautiful works produced in the Brussels workshops in the mid-16th century.

Throne-Room Door

This example of the German cabinet-maker's art dates from the second half of the 16th century and embodies splendid marquetry in various precious woods.

One of Philip II's Rooms

The rooms in which the King worked are furnished with an astonishing simplicity. On the table in this anteroom stands a fine 16th century timepiece, the most ancient in the royal collection. In the other rooms there is evidence of Philip II's scientific studies.

GERARD DAVID *(Oudewater, near Gouda, c. 1460 - Bruges, 1523):   Triptych, in Philip II's apartments*

The central panel of this Triptych, which belonged to Charles V, bears a *Descent from the Cross* (see detail on preceding page), a small oil painting that is one of the finest works of this master of Bruges. St John the Evangelist and St Francis of Assisi are depicted on side panels.

The King's Bedchamber ▶

Philip II's private apartments in the Escorial do not occupy a floor space of more than about 90 square yards, partitioned off to form three small rooms which are true monks' cells.   There is a study with windows affording a beautiful view through their leaded panes, and two very small, dark rooms, one of which serves as the King's bedroom.   From his bed, to which he was confined during an illness that lasted fifty days, Philip II could see the high altar of the church through a small private chapel.   Here the King died, on September 13, 1598, at the age of 71, after a reign of forty-two years.   In these small rooms with their whitewashed walls, decorated with blue Talavera tiles, and their tiled floors, can be found the most beautiful paintings and the most unusual objects of scientific study, including the exquisite watercolour studies of animals and plants by Albrecht Dürer.

Room occupied by Isabel Clara Eugenia

◀ Rogier van der Weyden: *Presentation of Mary in the Temple*

The predilection the Spanish Kings and grandees of Castile showed for Netherlands painting of the 15th and 16th centuries has resulted in the collection of countless masterpieces in the Spanish palaces and cathedrals by the great masters of a country which had close political and economic ties with Spain. One of the most favoured painters was Rogier van der Weyden, a preference which can be attributed to the pathos of the lively scenes which he painted and also to the clarity of his theological exposition. In accordance with his method of complementing the theme he was depicting by adding small scenes in the margins, Van der Weyden has placed John and St Anne in the centre of his great panel before a Gothic temple, the steps of which the child Mary, led by an angel, can be seen to climb. On either side of this, in small recesses, he has painted scenes from the life of the Virgin Mary. In circular panels on either side of the arch, we see a depiction of the Tree of Jesse and the Martyrdom of a Saint, beside which a worshipper kneels in prayer.

One of the Rooms occupied by Philip II ▶

Rooms occupied by Isabel Clara Eugenia

Isabel Clara Eugenia, daughter of Philip II and his third wife, Elizabeth of France, was the eldest and also the favourite daughter of the King and often accompanied him during his sojourns in the Escorial. She had three rooms at her disposal: a drawing-room on the north side of the palace and two bedchambers, both of which were connected to the altar of the church via a chapel. In its restrained elegance the Infanta's furniture, too, is in accordance with the style of living of 16th century Spain, though it is far richer than her father's furniture. The bed has a magnificent canopy of embroidered draperies. Especially beautiful is the portable organ, once in the possession of Charles V, a product of Flemish workmanship with rich and very delicate carving. On the walls are 16th century Flemish paintings (panels), including the large middle panel of a former triptych, *The Virgin and Child in a Mountainous Landscape*, which has been attributed to Orley. There is also a complete triptych, on the middle panel of which the Virgin Mary can be seen before a Gothic temple.

From the 18th century onwards these rooms, like those of Philip II, were no longer furnished. José María Florit furnished them for Alphonso XIII as they would have been at the time of Philip II, the Escorial's founder. Florit took as his guide the detailed information on the subject which Johan Lhermite, a servant of Philip II's, had left in his curious book entitled 'Le Passetemps'.

The Royal Library

It was Philip II's ambition to give the monastery he had founded a splendid library, and the beauty of the Escorial library, its sumptuous appointments and unique collection do indeed make it one of the most interesting libraries in Europe. Two arches supported by pillars built into the wall divide this large rectangular room into three sections. The paintings on the walls and ceiling are the work of Pellegrino Tibaldi, best of the Italian painters whom Philip II acquired to work on the Escorial. He must take credit for the frescoes in the large cloisters—the Courtyard of the Evangelists—and these in the library, on which he worked from 1586 to 1593. In the seven panels on the library's vaulted ceiling Tibaldi depicted the seven liberal arts and their patrons and, in the arch above the doorway, Theology with the four Fathers of the Church, (see also plate above). The grotesques in the Roman style were painted by Fabrizio Castello and Niccolò Granello. The bookshelves in the Doric style were designed by Juan de Herrera and were made, using precious woods from the New World and the Old, by Flecha, Gamboa, Serrano and other master-joiners. A special feature of this library is that the volumes stand with their spines to the wall and with their gilt edges facing outwards (see plate opposite). Philip II, a passionate bibliophile, collected books and costly manuscripts of all kinds. Despite the considerable losses sustained as a result of the great fire in 1671, the library contains—in addition to its 40,000 printed volumes — 1,900 Arabic manuscripts, 2,090 manuscripts in Latin and the Romance languages, 580 in Greek and 72 in Hebrew.

PELLEGRINO TIBALDI *(Puria, 1517 - Milan, 1594): Frescoes in the Great Cloisters and the Library*

In the galleries of the great cloisters round the Courtyard of the Evangelists there are thirty-three niches, which have been decorated with scenes from the New Testament. Those on the east side depict Jesus's Birth, Childhood and Acts. Those on the south side the Passion, and those on the west side Jesus's appearances after the Resurrection. These scenes were designed by Pellegrino Tibaldi, a master in draughtsmanship and of architectural perspective. According to Padre José de Sigüenza, the chronicler and eye-witness of the building of the Escorial, Tibaldi took pictures by Albrecht Dürer as his models. But the influence of Raphael and Michelangelo is obvious too. The harsh and monotonous colours do not do proper justice to the draughtsmanship. This was due to the King's impatience to see the work completed, which forced Tibaldi to make use of under-experienced assistants. Padre Sigüenza records that he had himself heard the artist complain of this. The Frescoes on the ceiling of the library (see detail above) are of greater merit, probably because Pellegrino Tibaldi had an outstanding painter to help him—Bartolomé Carducho (Florence, 1560 - Madrid, 1608).

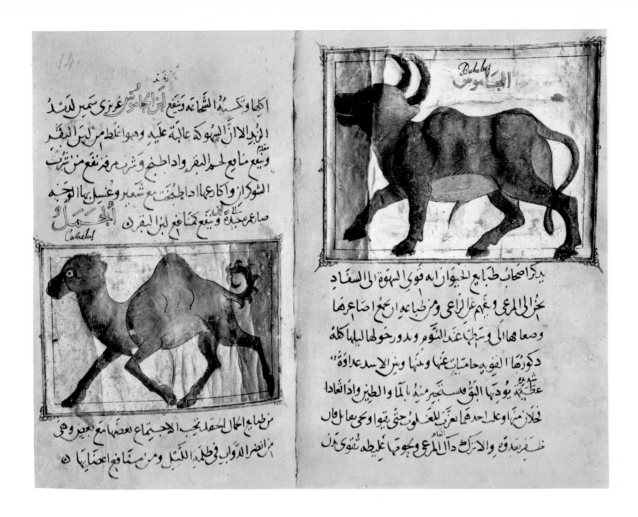

Illustrated Page from Turkish Manuscript – in the Library

The Escorial Library possesses numerous Arabic manuscripts, following a command of Philip III, that the collection of Mulei Zidan, Sultan of Morocco, should be lodged there. This collection had been taken by Rodrigo de Silva and Pedro de Lara as booty in 1611, during an attack on a Moroccan squadron.

An exquisite collection of illuminated manuscripts is on display in the showcases, including the 'History of Nature' by Ali ben Mohammed, dating from 1354 and containing excellent, unusually realistic illustrations. The text is in Arabic but the paper is of Turkish origin.

◄ ALONSO SÁNCHEZ COELLO *(Benifairón, near Valladolid, c. 1531 - Madrid, 1588): Padre José de Sigüenza – in the Library*

Padre José de Sigüenza (c. 1540-1606), a monk of the Order of St Jerome, was an outstanding historian and one of the most significant Spanish prose-writers of the 16th century. Philip valued him very highly and sought his advice, especially on the arrangement of the library at the Escorial. His portrait is a work of Alonso Sánchez Coello, a painter from Valencia, born in Portugal. Judging from the works of hiswhich Charles V and Philip II collected in Madrid and in the Escorial, he was a pupil of Titian. This portrait of Padre Sigüenza, masterly in its composition and its use of colour, is among the finest Spanish portraits of the age.

Mozarabic miniature painting in Spain during the 10th century, with its markedly oriental character, is among the most interesting work done in Europe at that time, and not only on account of its rich expression and radiant colours but also by virtue of its iconographical range, which had a powerful influence on Romanesque sculpture and painting. The *Codex Emilianense* derives its name from its provenance, the monastery of San Millán (San Emiliano) de la Cogolla in the Rioja region. Both the text, which comprises a collection of laws and conciliar decrees, and the miniatures are a copy of the *Codex Albeldense*, which was begun in 976 by an author by the name of Velasco.

Illuminated Page from the ' Las Cantigas' Codex of Alphonso X of Castile ▶

At his court Alphonso X the Wise, King of Castile and León (1252-1284), who was a great astronomer, jurist and poet, had collected the most gifted miniaturists, who transformed the manuscripts of his Works into true artistic jewels. The illustrations to his ' Cantigas '— songs of praise, in the Galician tongue, of the wondrous deeds of the Lady Mary — are the most significant of 13th century miniatures. The manuscript in the Escorial contains 1,257 scenes, framed by decorative architectural tracery in the Gothic manner, on 210 parchment pages.

Charles V's Prayer-book – in the Library

The explanation for the library's copious collection of manuscripts containing Dutch miniatures lies in the fact that the Kings of Spain were also the rulers of the Low Countries. Charles V's prayer-book consists of four parchment volumes, richly illustrated with contemporary miniatures, initial letters and margins. There are numerous portraits and coats of arms of the King, who from time to time also appears in it as one of the characters. According to Count Durrieu, a specialist on Dutch miniature painting, all the artists engaged on this work were Spaniards.

Pompeian Drawing-room in the Royal Palace

The first Spanish Bourbons, Philip V, Louis I and Ferdinand VI, felt at a loss when confronted with the excessively severe architecture of the Habsburg edifice. Charles III was the first to feel attracted to the Escorial. He was a passionate huntsman and saw in the royal palace an ideal centre for his hunting expeditions. But Philip II's palace was poor compared with the sumptuous Baroque palace of La Granja and an endeavour was made to embellish the interior. The walls were covered with tapestries—a large number of which came from the Madrid manufactury—based on designs by Maella, Bayeu, Castillo, Goya and other prominent painters, containing lifelike and colourful pictures of hunting scenes and popular customs. The Escorial's collection previously contained 338 of these tapestries, of which more than 250 are still in the building.

During the reign of Charles III the paintings of Pompei were rediscovered and the walls of one drawing-room in the Escorial were entirely covered with wall-hangings in the Pompeian manner. These were the work of José del Castillo and were based on sketches drawn by Raphael Mengs.

Ambassador's Anteroom in the Royal Palace

    This salon is decorated with some of the most beautiful tapestries made at the royal manufactury at Madrid. The designs were done by Francisco Goya and show his genius in the field of decorative painting. The series comprises: *The Maja and the Mummers* (1777), *The Kite* (1778), *Boys Gathering Fruit* (1777), *The Pottery Dealer* (1781), *The Boy and the Tree* (1779), *The Swing* (1778) and *The Washerwomen* (1780). In these works the forerunner of French Impressionism achieved a transparency and luminosity of colour that knows no equal. The other tapestries were based on designs by Bayeu and Castillo.

Francisco José de Goya *(Fuendetodos, 1746 - Bordeaux, 1828):* The Dance. *Tapestry in Dining-room of the Royal Palace*

Goya delivered the design for this on March 3, 1777, receiving 8,000 reals in return for it. It was woven in the succeeding years. Following the custom of the day, the figures, are dressed in the style of dandies and girls of fashion, of the ' majos de lujo ', as they were then called, their clothes being of brilliant, gay materials. The scene is laid in the vicinity of the Hermitage of San Antonio de la Florida, on the banks of the Manzanares. In the distance can be seen the dome of the church of San Francisco el Grande in Madrid.

◄ Francisco José de Goya: *The Maja and the Mummers (plate on page 92), The Washerwomen (plate on page 93). Tapestries in the Ambassador's Anteroom in the Royal Palace*

Neither of these tapestries communicates the beauty of the original designs, now preserved in the Prado. The craftsmen working in the royal manufactury at Madrid complained that it was impossible to reproduce the delicate strokes of Goya's brush. The background probably represents the ' La Casa de Campo ' park and the banks of the River Manzanares, near Madrid.

Dining-room in the Royal Palace

This humble and not very well-proportioned room owes its beauty to the splendid tapestries which adorn its walls. Two of these are works by Goya: *The Dance*, described on the preceding page, and *The Woodcutter*. Both were woven in 1780 expressly for hanging in this room. The others: *Country Vespers, Flower Girls, The Horchata Vendor, Vespers in the Venta del Cerero* and the *Bridge of Santa Isabel* are based on designs by Ramón Bayeu. The *Paseo de las Delicias* is by José del Castillo and there are others based on designs by G. Anglois and David Teniers.

Charles IV's Study in the Royal Palace

Compared with the relatively austere appointment of the rooms furnished during the reign of Charles III, those of Charles IV and Ferdinand VII are richly decorated. Every sort of exotic wood was employed and the costliest of precious metals, including platinum.

Work on the rooms extended from Charles IV's reign (1788-1808) to 1831, the sum invested in them reaching 28 million reals, a huge figure in those times. The floor, wainscoting and the King's bureau are of inlaid work in precious woods. Several craftsmen had a hand in the decoration, the last of them being Angel Maeso. The small landscape scenes, painted on copper and embedded in the marquetry of the wainscoting, were executed by Bartolomé Montalvo, the court painter. The walls are upholstered in sky-blue silk.

Exterior of the Prince's Pavilion

Their 'prince's pavilions' give the royal residences round Madrid a special charm. They are small pleasure palaces, usually standing slightly apart from the main buildings, pavilions in the style of the 'casinos' met with on the country estates of Italian princes. They have neither kitchens nor bedrooms, afternoon refreshments being the most that would be taken in them. They were also used for court parties. Their small, richly appointed rooms contain many priceless treasures.

The Escorial possesses two such small 'museums'— the Lower Pavilion and the Upper Pavilion. In 1772, Charles IV, then still Prince of Asturias, had the Lower Pavilion built in order to be able to escape there with his wife, Maria Luisa of Parma, and his gay companions from the all too strait-laced life at the court of his father, the 'Hunter-King'. The best Spanish architect the 18th century had to offer was chosen for the work—Juan de Villanueva (1739-1811), who had learned from Juan de Herrera's work how much architectural beauty depended on the scrupulous use of stone and on good proportions. The pavilion consists of a square tower with a Doric portico and two side wings.

Tower Room in the Prince's Pavilion

The rooms of the miniature palace contain countless valuable paintings, most of them small. In the Tower Room, the main drawing-room on the upper floor, hang oils by Guido Reni, Andrea Vaccaro and Luca Giordano. The elegant Pompeian grotesques with which the ceiling has been decorated are the work of Duque. On a small console table stands a statue of Charles IV in Carrara marble by Adan. The walls and the magnificent furniture are upholstered in blue silk. Very fine, too, is the chandelier. Its glass came from La Granja.

The Coffee Room in the Prince's Pavilion at the Escorial ▶

The white and gilt walls of this room are the work of Pablo and Mateo Bril. In the niches stand copies of Roman busts in Carrara marble. The miniature temple in the centre of the room houses a bust of Ferdinand VII.

The Blue Room in the Prince's Pavilion

The vaulted ceiling of the Blue Room was decorated with Pompeian grotesques by Gómez. On the walls hang paintings by Corrado Giaquinto, Luca Giordano and Francesco Solimena.

FRANCISCO JOSÉ DE GOYA: *Making the Powder* and *Making the Shot* ▶

The most important paintings in the Prince's Pavilion at the Escorial were two small oils by Goya, which depict episodes from the lives of the Spanish guerrilla fighters in the Sierra de Tardienta, during the war against Napoleon. Executed in 1815, they represent two masterpieces in the painter's œuvre, showing him at the very height of his powers. They are distinguished, above all, by their wonderful colouring and their technical perfection. The landscapes in the background are also very fine, revealing an extremely modern conception of painting. Today both paintings are to be found in the museum of the royal palace in Madrid.

The Upper Pavilion

Juan de Villanueva also built the Upper Pavilion. Here the Infante Gabriel, favourite son of Charles III, was to find recreation. He was a passionate lover of music, which explains why the small palace seems, in fact, more like a concert hall, attention having been paid, when furnishing it, mainly to the comfort of the audience and to the acoustics.

There is a magnificent view of the monastery and the sparse Castilian countryside from the park.

LA GRANJA DE SAN ILDEFONSO

At first sight it may seem absurd to speak of the Escorial and the palace and gardens at San Ildefonso, or La Granja, in the same breath. One can think of no two buildings more unlike each other than these two royal residences: two different ruling houses built them, the Hapsburgs and the Bourbons—poles apart in their politics and view of life. The severe sobriety of Philip II's palace contrasts sharply with the rather frivolous paganism of Philip V's, but the surrounding countryside could not be more different either. All the same—and this is what is so surprising—both edifices can be traced back to a very similar impetus. With the blood of Maria Theresa and Anne of Austria in his veins, Philip of Anjou, later Philip V, a grandchild of Louis XIV—who placed him on the throne of Spain—had inherited the physical and moral characteristics of the venerable imperial dynasty. Like his uncle, Charles II, who succeeded him, he was pious and weak-willed. More prominent in his temperament than the robust vitality of Henry IV of France or of the Sun King were the disinclination for state affairs and the melancholy of the last Spanish Hapsburgs. About 1720, prematurely aged and exhausted by the burden of power, he toyed with the idea of following the Emperor Charles V's example and abdicating in favour of his son, Louis, in order to retire to La Granja de San Ildefonso, as Charles V had done to the monastery of San Jerónimo de Yuste. Here, in the woods on the northern slopes of the Sierra de Guadarrama, was a Hieronymite monastery which he had discovered during a hunting expedition. He was charmed by its beautiful situation. It was thus that an ascetic impulse gave birth to this Yuste of the Bourbons, which to begin with was nothing more than a simple palace attached to a large church, but which in the course of time was to become one of the most splendid royal abodes in Europe.

It is a widely entertained fallacy to see something exclusively French in La Granja de San Ildefonso, as though it were rather like a Spanish Versailles. It is true, however, that this royal palace, with its gardens, its hunting preserves and its manufactures is the grandest and most impressive establishment of 18th century Spain and at the same time the most 'European', differing more than any other building from the Spanish version of Baroque and surrendering unreservedly to the great 'international' trend in the courts of the time. The picturesque royal residence at San Ildefonso is more reminiscent of the residences of German princes or of the country estates of Italian potentates than of the châteaux and parks of France, since it shares neither the distant perspectives nor the strict geometrical design of the latter. The name alone, La Granja—'country estate' or 'manor'—is characteristic of a specific era of European culture. In the constant struggle between the East and the West carried on on Spanish soil, La Granja de San Ildefonso, together with the aqueduct at Segovia and the cathedral at León, represents the greatest victory of Europe over the Celtic—Iberian and Moorish civilizations—civilizations which remained active in Spain even if now and then their influence had been concealed.

The royal residence with its gardens and woods lies on a slope in the watershed of two rivers, the Valsain and the Cambrones, which later join to become the Eresma. The lovely arrangement of gently descending gardens, with their architectural adornments and fountains, is dominated by a thickly wooded hill, known as 'the King's Chair'. To the south-east the backdrop is formed by the Sierra de la Atalaya, a bare mountain range with good stretches of meadowland and touches of furze and juniper between the rocks, and, on the other side of the valley of the Cambrones, by the massive chain of the

Sierra de Guadarrama with its peaks, Peñalara (c. 8,000 ft.), Sietepicos and Muerta, which are snow-covered for a great part of the year and on the slopes of which spreads the most beautiful pine-forest in all Spain. It is only in the south-west that the distant prospect of the high Castilian plateau is visible to the oberver, with the silhouette of Segovia in the foreground, seven miles from La Granja. San Ildefonso itself lies about 3,900 ft. above sea-level. This elevation and the humidity engendered by the many water courses and the dense woodlands explain why at La Granja the winter is protracted and very severe. But for a few days, spring is generally no more than a prolongation of the cold season. It is followed by a brief but brilliant summer and finally by a few splendid autumn days.

Elms, alders and ash-trees in the woods and oaks on the slopes—these are the species of tree that grow naturally here. When the gardens were being laid out, lime-trees, chestnuts, sycamores and various types of conifer were planted. From a certain elevation, about 4,500 ft. upwards, the stone-pine is dominant, a tree which achieves an astonishing size and splendour in this region. Thus geographical and climatic contingencies have produced the most beautiful countryside on all sides of the palace—the deep pine-wood, with its solemn shadows, the avenues, and the low-lying meadows or groves of oak-trees along the banks of the River Valsaín. But it was not so much the charm of the landscape that attracted the kings of Castile to this spot as the plentiful wild game. Red and fallow deer such as are to be found today only in the reservation near Riofrío roamed here until late into the 18th century, and also wild boar and wolves, which can still be found today in the Sierra, albeit in small numbers. In the Middle Ages even bears lived in the mountain forests near Segovia, to which many regional names are witness. From the 12th century onwards the monarchs handed over the woodlands along the banks of the Valsaín to the town council and nobles' representatives of Segovia, whilst retaining, however, the exclusive rights of the chase. It is plain that the ' House in the Woods '—a mere hunters' hut—existed as early as the reign of Henry III of Spain, a great huntsman. Henry IV, who loved the wildness and solitude of the forests, enlarged the ' House in the Woods ' and had several outbuildings put up. Then Philip II transformed the small hunting lodge into a palace in the manner of the Alcázar at Madrid, the Pardo or the Escorial, and his successors frequently stayed there until Charles II, as Ponz relates, ' on the last excursion he made here, after having gone scarcely a mile, saw that the palace was on fire—and in fact, as can be seen today, the entire west wing was burned down '.

In the year 1450, at a time when his father was still alive, Henry IV had a house and a hermitage built here in a charming setting, three miles or so from the old ' House in the Woods '. He dedicated the hermitage to St Ildefonso to mark, as it is said, his gratitude to the saint for having delivered him from an assault by a wild beast. At the beginning of their glorious reign, King Ferdinand and Queen Isabella presented the house and shrine, together with a few estates on the mountainside, to the monastery of Santa María del Parral in Segovia. In the mid-17th century, the Hieronymites, who had always been avid builders, erected on the site of the original buildings, then fallen into ruins, an estate and hostel, a solid construction of brick and granite. And so it was that ' La Granja de San Ildefonso ' came into being, designed as a summer residence for the monks of the Hieronymite monasteries, a place of reflection and contemplation, in a remote spot.

The deed of sale which Philip V agreed with the monks of Santa María del Parral, represented by their prior, Fray Andrés, was signed on March 23, 1720. Originally the King had only a modest residence in mind, to be constructed round the old monastery hostel, which was to be preserved to form the heart of the new building. Indeed, the heart of the palace at San Ildefonso is the former cloisters of the Hieronymite monastery—the Brunnenhof, with its walls of brick, its granite-columned portico, its granite cornices and corbels, and its beautiful baroque fountain. The building operations were put in the hands of Teodoro Ardemans, chief architect of the royal palace and of the municipality of Madrid. His conception owed much to the school of the later Hapsburgs, whose influence is clearly evident in the severe design of the north-east façade. A beginning was made with the work on April 1, 1721, under the technical direction of Juan Román. In this first phase, the palace seemed to be developing into a country residence such as the Hapsburgs had built for themselves in Valsaín, El Pardo or Zarzuela: white plastered brickwork, simple granite decoration and towers with slate-clad spires. In accordance with the pious aim of the foundation, the church was to stand in the centre, an edifice in the tradition of the Madrid churches about the year 1700. Thanks to an abundance of craftsmen, work went ahead rapidly on the modest palace and the extension of the ancient Hieronymite hostel, all the more so as, in the summer of 1723, the King and Queen paid almost daily visits to see how the building was progressing. Accordingly, it proved possible to have the new palace blessed on July 27, 1723, while that same year, on December 22, Cardinal Borja, the Patriarch of the Spanish Americas, was able to consecrate the church.

The design and splendour of the gardens strike a powerful contrast with the severity of the palace, the intention being that in this royal monastery they should provide a place of leisure and recreation. Here one will no longer find any trace of the traditional Spanish garden. When seeking spiritual refreshment in the life of retirement they were hoping to lead, the French King and the Italian Queen wished to be reminded of the parks of the châteaux of France and of Italian country estates. According to Antonio Ponz (1725-1792), a Spanish art historian, the King had called on an engineer named Marchan to see to the levelling of the site and the construction of the roads, and he evidently designed the lay-out of the gardens as well. The task of planting and decorating them was entrusted to a group of French experts, trained at Versailles, first under the supervision of René Carlier, who died in 1772, and later under that of Etienne Boutelou. Several Italian names occur, however, among the assistants. The statues, an indispensable item in this type of garden, follow the Versailles example in representing mythological figures—no great works of art, yet highly effective seen against the green shade of the trees or when reflected in the waters of the fountains. They are the work of several sculptors: René Frémin, Jean Thierry, Hubert Dumandré, Pierre Pitué, Jacques Bousseau and their assistants. The statues which stand on their own, distributed throughout the park, had to be executed in marble. It was desired originally to have the figures in the fountains, the vases and other decorations cast in bronze, and to this end Fernando Rey, a skilled craftsman, was sent for from Rome. Rey, however, quarrelled with the sculptors, who thereupon decided that a far richer and more artistic result would be achieved by casting them in lead. A lead foundry was installed at the palace at Valsaín.

The King was anxious to see everything completed quickly in order to be able to fulfil his intention. The year 1723 came to an end, however, and the palace was still not ready. Yet in the very first days of 1724 the King summoned the Marqués de Grimaldo, his private secretary, and the high-ranking court officials to his presence and informed them of his intention to abdicate in favour of his son, Louis, the Prince of Asturias, and to withdraw with his wife to La Granja. Actually, from that time on, the King and Queen lived with a reduced court at San Ildefonso, where they applied themselves to their devotions and to supervising the final stages of the building until, on August 31 of that same year, the young king, Louis I, died and Philip V remounted the Spanish throne. It was in this period that the collegiate monastery was founded, with an abbot, canons, and clergymen.

It was not until Philip V's second term as monarch that the royal palace at San Ildefonso acquired its European character and flowered in its full architectural splendour. It was no longer a question of a larger Yuste or a smaller Escorial but of the summer residence of the reigning monarch and his entire entourage.

The King himself, whose melancholia had now deteriorated into severe neurasthenia, submitted entirely to the taste of his second wife, Elizabeth Farnese, a passionate art-lover. In 1734 the old Alcázar in Madrid was burned down. The building of the Alcázar we know today was entrusted to the Abbé Filippo Juvara, a Sicilian and at the time the most important practitioner of the classical strain of European Baroque. It is possible that this same Abbé drew the design for the large façade of the San Ildefonso palace, the one on the garden side. After his death, his pupil, Giovanni Battista Sacchetti, took over his task. This imposing, fundamentally European edifice could stand equally well in Versailles or Turin, in Munich or Stockholm—the only Spanish note is in the warm hue of the stone, from Sepúlveda, which contrasts well with the white marble of the capitals, statues and trophies, the work of Barrata.

The King died on July 7, 1746 and was laid to rest in the collegiate church at San Ildefonso. When her stepson ascended the throne of Spain as Ferdinand VI, the widowed Queen withdrew once more to La Granja, taking with her her children, the Infante Louis, and the Infanta María Antonia, later Queen of Sardinia. The hunt-loving court of Elizabeth Farnese has been commemorated in a poem, *La Caza* (The Hunt), by Nicolás Fernández de Moratín (1737-1780). The work of building was continued without interruption. Still not content, Elizabeth Farnese—who was accused by all the princes of Italy of suffering from ' building mania '—now purchased the woodlands round Riofrío and had another splendid palace erected there. She died on July 11, 1766 and, like her husband before her, was buried in the collegiate church.

It was in Charles III's time that the royal palace of San Ildefonso acquired its definitive character. The furnishing is—at least in large part—the work of the ' Rey Arquitecto' and what was added after him is of little consequence. A tireless huntsman, the King found unending delight in the woods round Valsaín and Riofrío. Thus during the 18th and 19th centuries, La Granja was the Bourbons' summer residence, the royal palace forming the background to various crucial scenes in Spanish history.

On January 2, 1918, a fire broke out in the palace, destroying the roofs and causing serious damage on the first floor. After the royal residence had been restored to its former glory, in the apartments occupied by King Alphonso XIII and his consort, Victoria Eugenia von Battemberg, a Museum of Tapestries unique in Europe was set up, in which museum the finest specimens in the royal collection were put on display. The rooms, which have been preserved in their original state, contain — like all residences of the Spanish court—a fine collection of paintings, furniture, porcelain and other valuable works of art.

The Collegiate Church at San Ildefonso

Whereas the chapel of the château of Versailles is merely another component of the huge complex of buildings there, at La Granja the dome and towers of the church dominate the entire design and testify to the religious origin of a foundation which may appear secular to us today. King Philip V of Bourbon had received a papal bull from Benedict XIII by virtue of which the church was established as a ' Colegiata '. The designs were drawn up by Teodoro Ardemans, who had grown up in the artistic atmosphere which reigned at the court of Charles II. Yet according to Ives Bottineau, the palace's last chronicler, these designs were modified by the Italian Andrea Procaccini, who adapted them to conform with the prescripts of ' international Baroque '. The plan of the church is in the form of a Latin cross, at the four extremities of which are the main chapel, the prebendaries' choir and the two main entrances.

The Main Front of the Royal Palace ▶

In 1734 the great Sicilian architect Abbé Filippo Juvara was commissioned to build the garden front of the palace. After the death of the celebrated architect, his plans were carried out by his pupil, Giovanni Battista Sacchetti. It is known that the main façade was still not finished by 1739.

The Horseshoe Courtyard

On the one side, that of the 'Fama Parterre', the palace courtyard has been left open. Its name was to be a reminder, too, of the château of Fontainebleau with its 'fer-à-cheval' staircase. According to Bottineau, Sempronio Subiratti received the designs for the courtyard in 1737. They were probably the work of Andrea Procaccini.

The Fountain Courtyard ▶

Unlike the Horseshoe Courtyard, the Fountain Courtyard is entirely in accord with Spanish austerity and is reminiscent of the Escorial. It was built by the Hieronymite monks in the 17th century as the centre of La Granja, a place of meditation and recreation. Around it Teodoro Ardemans erected the small palace adjoining the church to which Philip V intended to retire when he had abdicated.

Interior of the Collegiate Church (page 114) ▶

The interior of the church of San Ildefonso is a masterpiece of 'academic' or 'international' Baroque, which differs strikingly from the extravagant Spanish-American Baroque style of architecture. The main altar was designed by Teodoro Ardemans and built by Juan Landaberi. The reredos is flanked by two pairs of Corinthian columns of blood-red marble with bronze capitals.

Processional Cross

The church of San Ildefonso possesses a wealth of tapestries, paintings, vestments and works of the goldsmith's art. One of the most beautiful items is the great Gothic processional cross of silver gilt, which came from the parish church of Santa Columba in Segovia. Many such crosses are to be found in the province of Segovia, which is renowned for its silversmiths. This specimen bears the mark of Antonio de Oquendo, a gold and silversmith who lived in Segovia around 1530.

Dining-room in the Royal Palace

In the dining-room hang paintings of the Flemish School, including flower-pieces, still-lifes and hunting scenes.

◀ *The Tomb of Philip V of Bourbon and Queen Elizabeth Farnese – in the Collegiate Church*

Philip chose as his last resting-place a chapel to the left of the High Altar, between the ' arms of the cross '. The walls are decorated in gilt stucco. The fresco on the vaulted ceiling represents the Cardinal Virtues, a work by Saxo. The sarcophagus stands on a socle of red marble. Above it, draped with a bronze pall on which rests a statue of Fama, is a pair of medallions bearing the portraits of the King and Queen, a work by the French artist Lebasseau. Behind rises a pyramid supporting an incense burner. The design and sculptures are the work of Hubert Dumandré.

The Marble Room in the Royal Palace

The marble room is one of the most sumptuous in the palace. It derives its name from the columns of Tuscany marble which decorate its walls. The shafts of the columns are of figured marble the socles and capitals of Carrara marble. The painting on the ceiling is by Bartolomeo Rusca.

Japanese Room in the Royal Palace ▶

A Japanese Room was constructed with wall columns and panels of Japanese lacquer. Four of the large panels have been filled in with oil paintings by Giovanni Paolo Pannini (1691-1765). These are probably his finest work. In settings formed by buildings of immense size, these paintings depict the following scenes: Jesus healing the Leper (signed in Rome, in 1736), Jesus and the Scribes (1736), Jesus being stoned for foretelling the Destruction of the Temple (1737) and Jesus driving the Money-lenders from the Temple (signed, but undated). The panels above the doors were painted by Locatelli and depict scenes from the Gospels.

View down the Gallery of Statues

Dining-room on the Ground-floor of the Royal Palace

The painting on the ceiling by Bartolomeo Rusca depicts the Rape of Proserpine.

The Throne Room in the Royal Palace ▶

Louis Michel van Loo *(Toulon, 1707 - Paris, 1771)*: *Elizabeth Farnese (above) and Philip V (right), portraits in the Royal Palace*

MICHEL-ANGE HOUASSE *(Paris, c. 1680 - Arpajon, 1730): Billiards*

Michel-Ange Houasse was the most important of the French painters which Philip V brought to his court. Strongly influenced by Italian painting of the day, he showed a preference for figures from the 'commedia dell'arte' in various attitudes and always in an Italian setting. In this picture we see the commedia dell'arte actors at the billiard table.

GIOVANNI PAOLO PANNINI *(Piacenza, c. 1691 - Rome, 1765): Jesus and the Scribes—in the Royal Palace* ▶

This large oil painting, signed in Rome and dated 1736, is one of Giovanni Paolo Pannini's masterpieces.

MICHEL-ANGE HOUASSE: *The Academy*

The paintings of Michel-Ange Houasse, the most important collection of which is to be found in the palace at San Ildefonso, are documents of inestimable value for telling us about life in Europe during the first half of the 18th century. The Academy shown in this work, which formerly hung in one of the palace drawing-rooms but was recently removed to the museum of the royal palace in Madrid, cannot be the Royal Academy of San Fernando at Madrid, since this was founded after the painter's death. It was probably an Italian academy, possibly the Art Academy at Parma, for the Duke of Farnese's coat of arms can be discerned above the niche with the statue of Hercules.

◀ GIOVANNI PAOLO PANNINI: *Jesus stoned for having prophesied the Destruction of the Temple*

Pannini revelled in scenes of great magnificence and put all his mastery into painting the perspectives of the architectural detail in his oils which adorn the Japanese Room at San Ildefonso.

129

FRANS SNYDERS *(Antwerp, 1579-1657): Stag Hunt*

The Spanish kings showed such a passion for painting that practically all the royal houses are veritable museums. At the palace at San Ildefonso the celebrated collection of tapestries and the no less famous gardens have put the not very extensive collection of paintings by French, Dutch and Italian masters in the shade. Among the principal items are the two large oils, *Stag Hunt (*see also detail, right) and *Wild Boar Hunt*, which have long been attributed to the painter Frans Snyders, from Antwerp. They originally hung in the royal palace at Riofrío, a famous royal hunting lodge about ten miles from San Ildefonso, which also possessed a considerable collection of paintings. King Alphonso XII had these two paintings removed to La Granja in 1881.

JACOPO AMIGONI *(Venice—possibly Naples—1675 - Madrid, 1752): Young Charles III receiving the Crown of Naples*

A brilliant decorative painter, a master at the composition of apotheoses and allegories and an eminent portrait painter, Jacopo Amigoni was one of the favourite painters of the Italian Settecento. One of his loveliest paintings, perfect in its draughtsmanship and lively in colour, is in the palace at San Ildefonso. It shows the Infante Charles, son of Philip V from his marriage with Elizabeth Farnese, being offered the crown of Naples by Apollo, Minerva and Neptune, whilst Fama announces the good tidings. The Neapolitan countryside is recognisable in the background. The occasion for the painting must have been the victory at Bitonto, which assured the Infante of the crown of the Two Sicilies.

St Jerome (Hieronymus) at Prayer – in the Tapestry Museum at San Ildefonso. ▶

This tapestry was made in the Brussels workshops in the early 16th century.

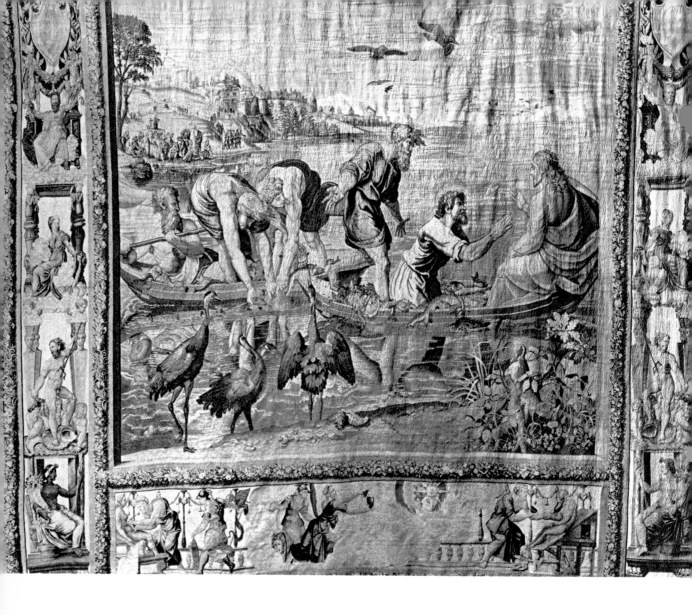

RAPHAELLO SANTI, *known as* RAPHAEL *(Urbino, 1483 - Rome, 1520)*: *The Miraculous Draught of Fishes—*
Tapestry in the 'Acts of the Apostles' Series, in the Tapestry Museum

Raphael's contribution to the art of tapestry weaving was to completely revolutionize the medieval style of tapestry. From now on what a 16th century Spanish scholar, Felipe de Guevara, called 'embroidered paintings' came into being. It was Pope Leo X who in 1514 commissioned Raphael to make the designs for this series, intended for the Sistine Chapel. The subject he proposed was 'The Lives of the Apostles Peter and Paul'. The series was woven at Brussels by Pieter Van Aelst, a chamberlain of Philip Le Bel and his son, Charles V. Of the many series woven on the basis of these cartoons, apart from those of the Vatican, one is to be found today in Berlin—it was originally intended for Henry VIII of England—and another in the royal palace at Madrid. One of the finest specimens in this series is on display in the Tapestry Museum at San Ildefonso.

Detail of a Tapestry in the 'Honour' Series – in the Tapestry Museum

This splendid series of large-scale tapestries, one of the most beautiful in the history of the art of tapestry weaving, was made in the Brussels workshops about the year 1520, as can be seen from the dress worn by the many persons depicted in it. It formed part of the wedding dowry of the Infanta María of Portugal, first wife of Philip II, whom she married in 1543. The ambitious aim of the collection was to portray the most prominent persons and their attributes in the Bible, Antiquity, and in Christendom during the Middle Ages. The dress worn is of the style affected at the Burgundian Court in the days of the Emperor Charles V. A shield on the first tapestry bears the following verse, explaining the meaning of the series:

Sacra Dei scriptura vocat veros ad honores
Quos tantum dignis virtus dispensat alumnis.

A composition as demanding as this required a man of considerable learning to devise the themes and the attributes of the figures involved, a great painter and a gifted tapestry-worker. Bernaert van Orley (c. 1492-1542) may have been the painter. The detail reproduced above shows Julius Caesar dressed as a German Emperor of the 16th century.

The Emperor Trajan and Entourage – detail from a tapestry in the 'Honour' Series ▶

Detail of a Tapestry in the ' Triumphs of Petrarch ' Series

According to Tormo and his assistants this series was probably woven about the year 1576 in Audenarde by Martin Cordier, using silk and wool. In each tapestry a carriage is portrayed with a Virtue or other allegorical figure pointing the way to Triumph. Here one sees the chariot of Fama (Fame) bearing a corpse out of whose mouth a sprig of laurel is sprouting. Below, a train of knights and ladies follow, carrying palm leaves in their hands.

◀ *Detail from a 16th century Brussels Tapestry – in the Tapestry Museum*

Tapestry in the ' Ape ' Series

This set of tapestries was made in Brussels by Wilhelm Thous ' the Elder ' in the 16th century.

The Pomona Fountain – in the Gardens at San Ildefonso

By its distribution of space, the Italian Baroque garden creates scenery of the greatest diversity, in which bronze statues or marble figures, enlivened by the play of water, represent myths and fables. Philip V entrusted the work of producing these figures to a group of sculptors which he sent for from Versailles: René Frémin, Jean Thierry, Hubert Dumandré, Pierre Pitué and Jacques Bousseau, together with several French and Italian assistants. Fernando Rey was persuaded to come from Rome to cast the bronze figures for the fountain. But when Rey proved unable to see eye to eye with the sculptors, the latter suggested to the monarch that to save time and money they should cast figures themselves in lead. Although the mythological figures of the La Granja de San Ildefonso are no masterpieces, they do blend perfectly with the landscaping of the garden.

The fountain illustrated here is the so-called 'Forest Fountain', a misnomer due to the mistranslation of the French word 'gerbe' (sheaf)—used on account of the sheaf-like appearance of the jets of water. The figures represent a scene from Ovid's 'Metamorphoses'. Vertumnus disguises himself as a woman in order to gain access to Pomona's flower garden. The central group is a work by the sculptor Thierry. The marble figures round the edge are by Doubou, Lagru, Cousa and Lebasseau.

◀ *Detail of 17th Century Brussels Tapestry – in the Tapestry Museum*

The Great Cascade of San Ildefonso ▶

The Fountain of the Three Graces

The great cascade before the main front of the palace is crowned with the Fountain of the Three Graces, a work of René Frémin.

The Horse-race ▶

Etienne Boutelou, one of the great garden architects of the Baroque Age, has provided the park of San Ildefonso with a number of distant prospects, all of which have the lovely Sierra de Guadarrama as a background. The most celebrated of these is a row of fountains known as 'The Horse-race'. It begins with three small basins : the two Snail Fountains and the Fan Fountain. Next is a large fountain with Neptune's chariot drawn by horses. On a terrace ten feet higher than the preceding group, comes the Apollo Fountain. Finally, rounding the series off, is the Andromeda Fountain, in which there is a statue of Perseus rescuing Andromeda.

The Aeolus Fountain (pages 146-147) ▶

This fountain is the work of René Frémin. The jets of water issue from the mouths of winged putti symbolizing the winds.

The Fan Fountain

This fountain, which owes its name to the fan-shaped jets of water that spout up from it, is one of the first three fountains in the 'Horse-race' group.

◄ *The Baths of Diana*

The Baths of Diana fountain is one of the most fascinating of all the fountains that are to be found in the gardens of European palaces. In its architectural design and to an even greater degree in the arrangement of the jets of water, it surpasses even the fountains of Versailles. It was constructed to designs by the architect Jacques Bousseau and with the co-operation of the sculptors Dumandré and Pitué. Its completion in 1742 marked the end of the works planned by Boutelou. It consists of a large wall of reddish stone and of graceful Baroque lines, in which, beneath a flattened arch, there is a niche. In the shelter of this niche sits Actaeon, the Hunter, spying on Diana and her nymphs whilst they bathe in the waters of the fountain. Jets of water spout up from among the group of bathers and these rebound from the wall behind to enclose the entire group in a dense mist of spay. The water flowing out of the uppermost basins falls in cascades down either side of the stone wall. On witnessing the spectacle for the first time, Philip V is said to have cried: 'You've amused me for three minutes, but you've cost me three million.'

The Basket Fountain

This fountain is not very rich in sculptures, but its cascades are all the more beautiful as a result, particularly when they are playing at full strength. By way of exception, no mythological story is represented here either. In the centre of the large circular basin rises a basket of flowers and fruit, supported by four swans. Around this group floats a garland of aquatic plants, on which the beautiful figures of two tritons and two nereids are raising themselves up. At times the jets of water which rise from the basket in the centre reach out several yards beyond the basin's rim.

The Frog Fountain

The marble and lead figures of the Frog Fountain again portray a scene from Ovid's ' Metamorphoses '. Latona, fleeing from the wrath of Juno with her children, Apollo and Diana, punishes the Phrygian peasants who refused her the water she begged of them for her children by turning them into frogs. In the centre of the circular basin, on a composite marble socle, Latona, also in marble, stands with her children and calls upon Heaven to punish the harvesters. In the water the heartless peasants can be seen going through the various stages of their metamorphosis. This composition, the work of René Frémin, is modelled on a fountain at Versailles, which takes the same myth as its subject matter.

Fama's Fountain

At the end of the loveliest garden of all rise the slender outlines of Fama, the Goddess of Fame's, Fountain (see detail, right), setting a fitting seal on the garden scenery. In the centre of a circular basin rises a mass of piled-up boulders—a favourite motif in the Baroque period. Towering on the top of these, Pegasus is about to take to the air, while Fama, mounted on the winged horse, points her trumpet to the heavens. With its unfortunate warriors trampled by the horse and tumbling down the rocks with their weapons, this makes a highly impressive composition. The sculpture is by Hubert Dumandré and Pierre Pitué.

This fountain was finished in 1740. With its perpendicular column of water rising out of the Goddess's trumpet and reaching a height of almost 150 feet, this work completes the display of fountains in the San Ildefonso gardens.

The Lake

In a tract of land left to the King in 1723 by the town of Segovia, on the slopes of the mountain which dominates the palace gardens, a reservoir was constructed, about 4,000 feet above sea-level. With its smooth surface, which for a great part of the year reflects the snow-capped heights of the Sierra, and with dense woods surrounding its shores, this is one of the main attractions in this uniquely beautiful and varied landscape. On the shores of the lake will be found a small landing-stage and two buildings. One of these is the Boathouse (Casa de las Barcas), the other the fish-breeding station set up in 1867 by Francisco de Asís, prince consort of Isabella II. From here the waters and ponds on the royal estates are reputed to have been colonized with trout from the Sierra de Guadarrama, a celebrated delicacy in Spain.

◀ Putto Riding a Swan – in one of the Fountains of the Eight Roads

As in most parks and gardens of this nature, in the gardens of San Ildefonso there is a rotunda, as though constructed for court concerts or parties. The one here is known as the Rotunda of the Eight Roads, since it forms the centre of a star described by eight avenues leading into the park. In the centre, on an octagonal socle of white marble, rises a group of statues by René Frémin; Mercury Bearing off Psyche to Olympus. Between each pair of roads is a fountain. These are handsome monuments, very similar as regards their architecture and only distinguishable from one another by the statues of the gods after which they are named and their various attributes. Beneath arches resting on Ionic columns, Neptune, Victory, Mars, Cybele, Saturn, Minerva, Hercules and Ceres stand reflected in the fountain waters. Winged putti ride on swans from whose beaks, water spouts.

The Royal Gondola

The artificial lake, popularly referred to as 'the sea', was originally constructed to supply the fountains in the royal gardens with water. The court also used them for fishing, boating and water fêtes. It was for these that the gondola with its rich Baroque ornamentation was used, the vessel now being on display in the boathouse on the shore of the lake. The sides of the gondola are decorated from bow to stern with rich reliefs composed of tritons and nereids at play. The roof over the King's seat, reminiscent of Venetian gondolas, is supported by mythological marine figures in the manner of caryatids. The hull is painted black, the ornamentation being gilt.

The winged lion which serves as the figurehead may have caused the editor of Murray's 'Handbook for Spain' to think that the gondola was a present made to Philip V by a Doge of Venice. Others have seen a connection between the reliefs and the carving on the coaches in the famous 'Museu Nacional dos Coches' near Lisbon, believing that the gondola was a gift from King John V of Portugal. However, it was probably built for the King in the palace workshops. In 1872 King Amadeo I of Savoy had it restored.

INDEX

ACKNOWLEDGMENTS

Istituto Geografico De Agostini, Novara: 31, 34, 55, 58, 59, 60, 61, 67, 70, 83, 92, 124.

Loren, Madrid: 11, 14, 15, 16, 17, 18, 19, 20, 21, 22, 24, 25, 26, 27, 28, 29, 37, 38b, 39, 40, 41, 42, 43, 44, 45, 46, 47, 50, 52, 53, 68, 69, 71, 72, 73, 74, 77, 79, 80, 81, 84, 87, 88, 89, 90, 91, 95, 96, 97, 98, 99, 100, 102, 112, 113, 114, 115, 116, 117, 120, 121, 126, 127, 129, 132, 134, 135, 138, 139, 141, 144, 146-147, 149, 150, 152, 153, 154, 155, 156.

Mas, Barcelona: 23, 32, 33, 35, 36, 38a, 82, 85.

Scala, Florence: 12, 13, 30, 48-49, 51, 54, 56, 57, 62, 63, 64-65, 66, 75, 76, 78, 86, 93, 94, 101, 109, 110-111, 118, 119, 122-123, 125, 128, 130, 131,133, 136, 137, 140, 142-143, 145, 148, 151.

DATE DUE
